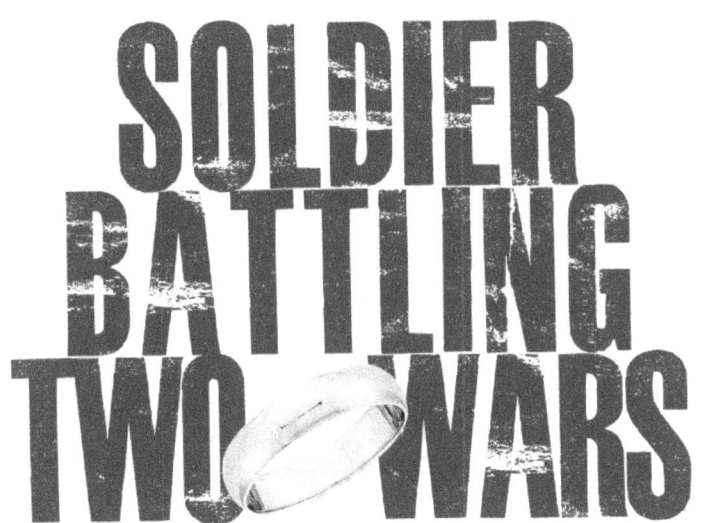

SOLDIER BATTLING TWO WARS

THOMAS JAMES LOTT, JR.

HOV
PUBLISHING

Soldier Battling Two Wars

HOV Publishing a division of HOV, LLC.
www.hovpub.com
hopeofvision@gmail.com

Cover Design: Hope of Vision Designs
Editor/Proofread: Phyllis Miller-Bridges for Harvest Seed

Contact the Author, Thomas James Lott, Jr. at:
thomaslott69@yahoo.com

For further information regarding special discounts on bulk purchases, please visit www.hovpub.com

ISBN Paperback: 978-1-955107-73-0
ISBN eBook: 978-1-955107-72-3

10   9   8   7   6   5   4   3   2   1

Printed in the United States of America

Dedication

I dedicate this book to freedom, life lessons, God's ever abounding love, grace and mercy, and the power of self-love.

Thank You

I am free of the ills and bonds that for a time held me as a person and kept me from being my best self. I have learned valuable lessons from situations, wrong choices, and mistakes I made, and the choices of others towards me, even as far back as my childhood. God has forgiven me and healed many wounds of my heart and mind. God loved me and never left me, even when I departed from Him. Love for God and learning to love myself has given me a new lease on life and a hope that I didn't always have.

I have come a long way from the little boy that always wanted to be with his mom, and the teenage that found trouble while trying to find himself, and young husband, father, and soldier. By much mercy and grace and though with scars, cuts, and bruises, The Soldier Fighting Two Wars, survived the battles. Realizing how things could have gone another way, leaves me ever humbled and so grateful.

Last, to those who are the joys of my life and the source of my heart's beat, you know who you are and how much I love and appreciate and thank you!

Content

Chapter 1

HUMBLE BEGINNINGS

Hello, my name is Thomas James Lott, Jr. I was born on June 25, 1969, in Ocilla, Georgia. I am the second born of six children. Isn't it weird for the second born son to be his father's junior? In the pages to follow, I will share my life with you from a husband and a soldier's perspective.

Life was never that hard, but not that simple either for me or my siblings. I can't remember too much of my childhood, but I do remember living in the small town of Willacoochee, Georgia with my grandmother on my father's side. My mom and father would eventually separate and get divorced. My mom moved to New Jersey for a while and eventually we ended up in the small town of Alamo Georgia, which is south of Atlanta.

My grandmothers were incredibly special in my life. I always looked forward to seeing them and my father when we visited. Me and my brothers would play on the railroad tracks behind my grandmother's house. I was always one of those kids that tried to stay away from trouble. Nevertheless, trouble would eventually come alone. Everyone there embraced us with open arms and believed in the saying, "It takes an entire village to raise a child."

I can't recall how old I was when we settled in Alamo, Georgia. I do remember starting kindergarten, which required you to be at least five years old. Eventually, my mom remarried and that is when my life began. As I grew old enough to help around the house with chores and everything else, I found myself bonding more and more with my grandfather. He allowed me and my brother to help him with cutting yards after school and on the weekends.

I didn't grow up in a home where we hugged, said I love you, or congratulated each other when we did good at home or school. My wife taught me how to show love to our children. A hug felt very weird. I was ashamed that I didn't know how to show love. As I matured, to keep us busy and out of trouble, my grandfather passed the yards off to one of us to maintain. As the years passed me and my brothers shared the task of cutting people's yards, which we worked faithfully.

At a noticeably young age, I got involved with sports and girls. I lost my virginity very young; I was somewhere around 11 to 13 years old. I had no clue what I was doing! I just did what I was told and what I'd been exposed to. I remember, we had a neighbor who had the same number of kids as my mom. We would play together and fight one another on a regular basis. Fighting wasn't for me, but I had to learn if I wanted to hang out in the neighborhood. Whippings were received on the regular with me and my brothers.

As they say, boys will be boys. When my mom was at work, I would sneak girls into the house after school.

My mom worked day and night shifts, so there were times when we were home alone, but most of the time we had a babysitter. She was a very hard-working woman. She never allowed us to hang in the streets with the other kids. She would say if the streetlights came on and we weren't home yet, the doors to the house would be locked. I slept in my mom's car plenty of nights; luckily her car doors were unlocked.

During my childhood, like most kids, I did things that were not right. As time went by, I began to find myself getting into trouble. This was mainly because I felt that my mom didn't care about my accomplishments or the positive things that I was involved in, so it became easy for me to not care as well. I remember wanting to go to a football game and my mom wouldn't give me any money to go. So, I decided to go to a lady's house whose yard I maintained to ask if she had any work for me. There wasn't much work that day, still she told me to throw away some old checkbooks that were in your storage closet. I decided to rip one out before throwing them away. I didn't know how to fill out a check, I did the best I could and tried to cash it. Unfortunately, I was caught and was taken to my grandparents' house because I wouldn't give them my mom's name. I ended up going to court. However, because I didn't have a criminal record and I was very good in school, I was given six months of probation. That woke me up quickly! I was just a kid and had never been so scared in my life. When the judge asked my name, I couldn't even hear myself speaking.

On another occasion, me and a friend wanted some grapes and decided to go into this man's yard and pick grapes without his permission. He came out with a gun to scare us and make his point clearly known. We were almost shot! Luckily, he didn't press any charges. He just told us to stay out of his yard.

I remember us having numerous babysitters, which took a toll on me mentally. None of the babysitters mistreated us, but they all had different personalities and different levels of tolerance. By the time you got used to the babysitter, there was a new babysitter. Being a young boy, I always wanted my mother's attention.

Chapter 2

GROWING PAINS

I played football and basketball with my friends in the neighborhood and at school. My stepdad would get me and my two brothers together and have us play basketball with him and his friends. Saturdays and Sundays were the days to play ball in our yard. The years seemed to fly by. While in high school, I continued to be very sexually active. I dreamed of becoming a police officer one day. As I played sports for my school, I never saw my mom at any of my games. Everyone else's parents would be there except mine. I always wanted my mom to see me play because her opinion mattered to me.

One day, while standing outside of some apartments, this female walked across the street to the school. My friend bet me $5 that I couldn't talk to her. I accepted his bet and the next day at school, I wrote her a letter and gave it to her. She took the letter home to her mom. Her mom wanted to meet me to see who was trying to talk to her teenage daughter. Even though there was a big age gap between us, her mom approved of me dating her daughter as long as I followed her rules. At the time she was 13 and I was 17 years old.

So, in 1986, my junior year in high school, we officially started dating. Don't let me forget to mention she was also the sister of one of my high school friends. Three months later, we became sexually active. At that moment, I found out that I wasn't her first sexual encounter. She had a boyfriend before me, and they had already been active. I took on the role of providing for her every need until she graduated from high school. Whenever my mom cooked, she would have me bring her a plate. She wasn't deprived of food at her home, it was just my way of doing what she asked of me.

My senior year I was voted Mr. FHA and Best Dressed in my high school. Our relationship was off and on throughout my senior year. I recall buying her class ring, but her mom told her to give it back because she was going to buy it for her. Sadly, she never received her class ring.

I remember the time she slapped me so hard in front of her mom. All I could do was sit there and take it. Our relationship started out with a big bang, but after that slap things changed. She claimed that I gave her an STD when she was a senior in high school, and I had already graduated. We both were treated for the disease. I blamed her and she blamed me. Neither one of us would own up and take the blame for that incident. I took her to the prom even though we were not together. After the prom, I took her home, and left to pick up another friend-girl to finish off my night.

Once I graduated in 1988, I planned to join the military, but my mom didn't want me to join. She convinced me to stay home, get a job, and help her. I was stuck in a small town without hope for a brighter future. All I had to look forward to was working at a factory of some sort. I found myself jumping from one job to the next. To top it off, my girlfriend was pregnant with our first child. I ended up losing numerous jobs due to layoffs.

Chapter 3

RESPONSIBILITY & IRRESPONSIBLE CHOICES

Eventually, I found myself working the streets selling drugs. Now I was doing something illegal to meet my financial needs. I had a baby to take care of, and a car payment. I always had the ambition to do what's right, but we all must eat. Things were getting worse every single day. Things had gotten so bad, I had my girlfriend dropping drugs off wherever and whenever. I must say this much, you never know who is doing drugs until you are in that line of work. Money began to come from every direction.

I recall the time when my best friend came to my girlfriend's house and asked me to ride to Valdosta with him and his girlfriend's brother. For some reason my girlfriend said that I didn't spend time with her and she didn't want me to go. So, I didn't go with them and stayed with my girlfriend. Later, I got word that my friend had been shot and killed in McRae, Georgia. I was in total disbelief and said it had to be his brother that was shot because he went to Valdosta. Unfortunately, he never made it to Valdosta. I went to pay my respect to his family, and everyone was in tears. I was with his family when he was taken from the hospital to a hearse.

I couldn't believe that my best friend was no more. I took it upon myself to find those that killed him. God had to have his hands on me because I never found them. I tried my best to get him to go into the Army with me on the Buddy Enlistment Program. His family asked me to speak at his funeral. This was a very sad moment in my life.

It was then that I knew without any doubt, I had to leave that small town and make something of myself and support my family. The money I was making and the compensation I received from losing my job went toward my daughter even before she was born. I didn't want to fail as a father. Every dime I had was put into her birth. She was born on 31 January 1989. I was not able to make it to the hospital for the birth of my daughter. The night my girlfriend went into labor, I was home asleep, but no one heard anyone knocking on our house door. To this day, she still says I was with a female and not at home.

I finally got to the hospital early that morning to discover that my daughter was born with a very rare condition, Larsen Syndrome. This is a disorder that affects the development of bones throughout the body, and normally presents with the dislocation of all joints. With the stress of life already bearing down on me, I had another issue to deal with on top of everything else. My daughter needed special care and special doctors to take care of her needs.

As a father, I did everything possible to support my girlfriend, myself, and my daughter. I let my girlfriend keep my car while I was at work so that she had transportation. My daughter would stay with me some nights so that my girlfriend could get some much needed rest. Her mother was very kind to me and treated me like I was one of her own.

During her senior year in high school, she broke up with me to enjoy her summer and experience new people. I agreed and moved on with my life as a single young man. I didn't realize she was going to cause major problems whenever she saw me with other females. She would try to intimidate them by confronting them with her cousin. I tried to do the same to her whenever I saw her with her male friends.

There was never a dull moment with her for the entire summer. While out with one of her male friends, she was in a car accident and my daughter was in the back seat. I was not informed of this tragic event. I was at a city 4th of July event, when her cousin just happened to see me there and told me what happened. Being the person that I am, I went to her cousin's house to check on her. I ended up sleeping on the floor and holding her hand as she slept on the couch. She had bandages on her face for a very bad cut. I woke up the next morning and went home.

Time went by and I was still with my friend-girl. We were at a softball game where she was playing, and my ex-girlfriend started the ruckus again. She showed up and asked me to go with her and give her some good sex because her friend wasn't getting the job done. I refused. Next thing I knew, she was handing me my class ring and some of my other jewelry. I wondered how she got her hands on my jewelry. Well, my friend-girl had been wearing my jewelry and unfortunately, her friend was holding the jewelry for her while she played softball. Her friend was also my ex-girlfriend's friend. Just as I noticed I was missing a necklace, she left to go to the store, and I went behind her. Then I saw that she was wearing my necklace. I grabbed her and snatched it from around her neck. Suddenly, I felt a punch in my back. As I turned around to see who hit me, I decided to walk off and not make matters worse.

She didn't go back to the game. She did however tell her stepdad that I hit her, which I did not. When I got back to the game, I was quickly surrounded by a crowd of people who thought I hit her. I was in a situation where someone could get hurt or possibly even worse. One of them had a screwdriver! I stood there defending myself with words... I made it very clear that I was not afraid of any of them and if anyone got hurt, it would not be me! Good thing, a very close friend of mine was there to deescalate the situation.

After this incident, we had to speak with a probate judge because she wanted to take a warrant out on me and put me in jail. Luckily, the judge understood it was a lover's quarrel and was able to talk some sense into us.

Chapter 4

A HUSBAND & SOLDIER IS BORN

I had taken the Armed Services Vocational Aptitude Battery (ASVAB) for the Army and was waiting on my movement date for basic training at Fort Dix, New Jersey. My mom convinced me to talk to her and try to work things out between us. We ended up getting back together and six months later, I was in the Army. Now, I was trying to become the best I could be, while dealing with the pressure and issues of a relationship and raising my daughter.

I can't remember exactly when I asked her to marry me, but it was somewhere between basic training and advanced individual training. Once I graduated from basic training, she and her family drove me to Fort Belvoir, Virginia to continue my training. It was a very trying moment for her. She thought of the abundance of female soldiers there, how far away she would be, and was afraid that temptation would get the best of me. As she began to cry, I comforted her as much as I could. I told her everything was going to be alright and how much I loved her and only her.

Midway through my training, I flew home for the 4th of July weekend to marry her. It was a beautiful sight to see her in her wedding dress. The night before the wedding, we made love and that's when my second daughter was conceived. The next morning, I flew back to Virginia to continue my training.

When I graduated from Advanced Individual Training, I went home for at least 10 days to spend time with my new family and friends. After visiting with them, I flew out to Fort Hood, Texas to begin my career as a soldier. Once I was established and found a place for my family, my wife joined me. It was our first time ever being on our own and away from our families. It took a terrible toll on us. We were homesick, especially her. We managed to get ourselves together and prepare for the birth of our second daughter.

Before she was born, we went home to visit family and friends. One of my wife's high school classmates came back with us to help her because she was in her third trimester. Our new baby girl was born on 14 March 1993. My mother-in-law drove up to visit us and meet her second granddaughter. She asked to take the baby with her until we were able to get ourselves more established. We allowed both girls to go with their grandmother, but letting our baby go at such an early age was hard on my wife.

With both of our daughters in Georgia, we had a lot of time on our hands. I would hang out with my friends and enjoy the clubs and barbecues, while she stayed at home. She wasn't a club person, nor did she drink. There were times when I would come home, and she would have the chair propped against the door so I couldn't get into the house. Eventually, she made friends with our neighbor across from us and started hanging out with her. Even though we were very young, and our marriage was new, I was very faithful to my wife. I didn't do anything to violate or disrespect the vows we took on 3 July 1992.

In the Army, you are subject to work long hours, you must do whatever it takes to complete the mission. This quickly became a fact of my life. We trained for weeks at a time, which caused me to be away from my family for long periods of time. One day, I told my wife that I had to be gone from home for at least a week or two to support a unit in the field training. I packed my bags, gave her a kiss, and was off to do training. After a few days, we were told we could go home, but with the understanding that we needed to keep our phones close by because we could be called back at any time of the day or night.

When I got home, she was not there. As I got settled, I called our neighbor to see if she was there, and he said yes. I told him, "Don't tell her that I'm home, I want to surprise her because she thinks I'm still in the field training." He agreed not to say anything. As we continued to talk, I heard my wife ask him who he was talking to. Quickly, I told him not to say my name and to give her one of his friend's name, which he did. She responded, "Tell him my husband is in the field for training, I need him to come by so I can ride his big ass." I was in total shock, and so was he.

.

Now, I was expecting her to come back and say she was only joking or something, but she never did. I told him not to say anything, I would handle it when she came home. Finally, when she walked through our apartment door, she was shocked and surprised to see me sitting there. She asked, "Baby, when did you get home?" I replied, "Don't worry about that, so when is he coming over so you can ride his big ass? She was in disbelief and couldn't believe what I was saying. I told her that it was me on the phone with our neighbor. Then she began to explain that she was only joking. I asked her how could she joke like that in front of our friends and never correct herself. I told her if it had been someone else on the phone, he would have come over.

Her explanation was just not acceptable. I did what anyone would have done at that age in my situation, I put her out. She called her mom, and her mother said if I didn't want her daughter to send her back to Georgia. When I told her mom what she said, there was complete silence. She went to stay with one of the noncommissioned officers and his wife. The next day he showed up at my apartment to let me know where she was, and that regardless of who was wrong, I needed to apologize to her. I did what I was told, and she came back home.

Chapter 5

TWO WRONGS NEVER MAKE IT RIGHT

Eventually, we decided to move into a bigger place, especially since our daughters were back at home with us. As time went by, we were doing well. For the first time in our marriage, we felt like a real family. We had barbeques, parties with friends, and we were enjoying life to the fullest.

Then one day, I got a phone call from my wife's friend, our old neighbor whose house my wife would go to. She tells me that her fiancé told two women that he had sex with my wife when we lived in the apartment across from them. I couldn't believe it, here we go again with this bull! I was practically exploding! Then she asked me to meet her at her job. When I arrived, my wife was already there and in tears. Once we finished talking, she continued to deny any wrongdoing and stuck with her story. Our old neighbor called off her engagement and left the state of Texas.

That same night, my wife wanted me to confront the guy. So, with my pistol in tow in the holster, I confronted him. He tells me, "I don't know what they are talking about." I said, "You described to them the nightie she had on to a tee; now you mean to tell me these girls are lying on you!" He couldn't even look me in the eyes anymore, he just sat there quietly.

From that day forward, I decided I was going to start doing me regardless of what it may cost me. Throughout my military career, I had numerous affairs. I completed 26 years of military service and for at least 23 of them, I was unfaithful to my wife. There were women she believed and claimed I had been with, and some of them I had, and others I had not.

While I was stationed at Fort Hood, I began to cling to this Staff Sergeant, who took me under his wing and mentored me. He was much older and would babysit for us when we wanted to spend some time together. I remember the day I had to call him to come to our house because my wife was after me with a knife. I had to lock her in the house until he showed up. He talked to us and told her she was stupid for trying to cut me. Unfortunately, years later while still serving in the military, my mentor died at Fort Stewart, Georgia.

Later, I was stationed at Fort Gordon, Georgia. Initially, we were staying in different cities, while I looked for a place for us to live. We were both having affairs during this time apart. Then my wife began to have some female issues. In the past, she always blamed me if she experienced any of these problems, but this time it wasn't because of me. We were both tested for STDs. She was upset and immediately ready to leave the office when the doctor gave us the results.

The Army was our income and without it, we would have been out on the streets with two kids struggling to make ends meet. My wife worked, but it was not enough to support our family. To put it mildly, we were living foolishly, especially knowing that the Army had zero tolerance for spousal abuse and adultery. I could have been punished, loss money, and loss rank. Still, we were not taking any precautions to prevent being found out. Thank goodness, my superiors did not know how bad things had gotten between us.

Her brother would come visit us at Fort Gordon, and we visited him in Atlanta. We would occasionally go to FreakNik in Atlanta. I recorded the event one year. When my wife watched the tape, she confronted me about the video. It showed me lifting a girl's dress while she was dancing for the camera. I didn't mean any harm, I was just having fun and enjoying the event.

On another occasion, I went to a party, she showed up and automatically thought I was there with a female. She threw her keys at me and hit me in my face. I was so upset and embarrassed. I threw a beer bottle at the wall, then grabbed her around her neck and held her until she passed out. There she laid on the ground, with my friend hovering over her to make sure she was okay. Still upset, I got in my car and went home. Her mom was there with the girls; she asked what was going on and I told her. My wife also said that I pushed her down the stairs, but I have no recollection of that at all.

She called the police. They came and questioned me to get my version of what happened. He saw there was blood and scratches on my face, which were caused by the keys she threw at me and asked if I wanted to press charges against her. I told him, "No, just let her leave." She loaded up her car and left with our kids and her mother. Now, I was calling continually, trying to talk to her and see how my girls were doing. Eventually, her grandmother told her to call me because I was worrying her to death calling so much. After we finally talked, she decided to return to Fort Gordon and work things out.

As time went on, I received an assignment in Europe. When we arrived in Germany, it was beautiful and exciting. However, it didn't take long before she started accusing me once again of having an affair. It seemed like it would never end; she would always put me with a woman. Here we were in this beautiful country and the devil was still working his magic.

Once, she took a lug wrench from the trunk of her car and struck me with it. She was becoming very violent. She would call the military police to our home, and I would always have to leave for 72 hours. At every station I was at this would happen. Remember, I never laid a hand on her when this was happening. That's the power a spouse must have when you are in the Armed Forces.

The Armed Forces job is to protect their investment at all costs, the soldier is the investment. I have seen a lot of soldiers lose their career because of a spouse's phone call to their chain of command. As a soldier in the Armed Forces, you are guilty until proven innocent. It seems as if you are never right but always wrong in any situation. I didn't want that to happen to me, so I played along with her shenanigans.

In time, my unit received an assignment in Saudi Arabia. While I was in Saudi Arabia, she was home going to parties in the single soldiers' dorms. I was doing what I normally did, finding companionship elsewhere. There I was in a foreign country, thousands of miles away from my family, and she was running the streets.

I returned from Saudi Arabia as a young noncommissioned officer. In addition to dealing with the stress at home, I was now dealing with other soldier's problems as well. I went home on leave to visit my family and found myself in the bedroom of another woman. Her ex-boyfriend saw me and immediately started spreading the word. When I arrived home in Germany, she had already gotten the bad news. She asked me about it, and I told her the truth. "Yes, I was in her room, but nothing happened." She confronted the female, and she told her the exact same thing.

Chapter 6

NEW BEGINNINGS

Still in Germany, my wife begins to go to church and gives her life to Christ. I finally started to attend church and gave my life to Christ also. I became a totally different person. I stopped drinking, clubbing, and entertaining other women. I put all foolishness aside and focused on us. My family and marriage were my sole priority. I became very active in the church and was appointed to Deacon. It felt as if nothing could stop us from growing spiritually. In my eyes, though we had plenty of room to grow, everything was nearly perfect. Our marriage was doing great!

Now, after a three-year tour, I was headed to an assignment in Colorado Springs. During the transition, I took 30 days leave for us to spend time with family and friends before we headed to my next assignment. While we were home, we got into a big argument at my mom's house. My mom took my wife to her room and talked to her about a rumor that was out there saying one of my daughters belonged to another man. After hearing this, she went to her mom's house and shared the news with her. I must admit, I didn't know what to believe because of how toxic our marriage had been. Regardless of it being true or not, how was I supposed to handle news of that magnitude?

What my wife never understood was that I was no different than her. I had feelings, emotions, and a heart that was hurting also. There was always something going on within our marriage but somehow, we would pull it together and continue to move forward with pain and all.

After my leave, I left for my next assignment, which was at Fort Carson, Colorado. While there alone, I gave into loneliness and had an affair. I recall the day that I called my wife crying. When she asked what was wrong, I told her I started drinking again but couldn't bring myself to tell her why I started drinking again. The truth was drinking had become my escape from the guilt and shame I felt after falling so far from where I was in God and having another affair. I was so hurt and disappointed in myself. I didn't have a church family or a church that I attended there. I read my bible daily, hoping that would be enough. I tried with everything in me to fight off the old ways and urges I had abandoned. The devil knew my weaknesses…

One night after my family joined me, while I was getting ready to go to the club, my wife looked through my wallet and found an email address, which belonged to the women that I had been unfaithful with. When she asked me about it, I told her about the affair. She was very disappointed and went to take a bath. When I went to the bathroom, she was sitting in the tub crying. I apologized several times, trying to assure her that I didn't mean to hurt her. She wanted me to show her how I had been with the other women. I told her that I only had sex, I didn't make love to her, and didn't show her. I knew that would only make her hurt more. Although, we didn't have marriage counseling, we weathered the storm once again and managed to stay together.

Time went on and while there, we conceived and had our third child. Due to stress in our marriage, he was born at 28 weeks. The day my wife and son came home from the hospital, she found a letter on the dresser in our bedroom that I had written to a female. I meant to throw it away but forgot. It wasn't a love letter; it was just a letter thanking this certain female for her friendship during some of the difficult times of my marriage. See, before our son was born, I moved into the military barracks to escape the pressure of my marriage. This female was a fellow soldier that I met at work. We would confide in each other and offer support to each through tough personal situations in our lives. Our friendship lasted about a year. Once back at home and after my son's birth, I convinced my wife to start drinking with me because she was no fun, and she didn't know how to dance. She needed to loosen up.

Once I was deployed to Iraq, my wife began to have an open affair in Colorado and Georgia. I wish war on no man or woman. Now, I was a soldier battling two wars, one for my marriage and the other for my country. I was away from my family for 11 months. During that time, I couldn't take rest and restitution, because I arrived 30 days after my unit. I didn't know if I was going to make it back home to see my family, so I survived the best way I knew how. I called and wrote home as often as I could, but it always seemed like it was never enough. There I was in Iraq, and on some occasions when I called home, we would argue about me not calling enough. She didn't understand the way the system worked when calling home. We had a long line of soldiers, all trying to call their loved ones on just three phones. I tried my best to stay grounded, but it was hard. Once again, I began to go back to my old ways. I started drinking alcohol, which was prohibited. The Iraqis that worked in our camp would provide it for us. Some days were quiet, and others were hectic. Many nights, I cried myself to sleep; until I began to find comfort in someone else's arms.

When I returned from Iraq, my wife and I were discussing the rumors I'd heard about her and some guy, when she received a call from the guy in Georgia. I looked at her phone and said, "That's him calling now, answer it!" She casually stated, "Why is he calling me anyway?" I asked her to pull up her phone account and open it so I could see her incoming and outgoing calls. She refused. Later, I found out that sometimes when I called her from Iraq, she was in the club and would go in the bathroom to answer the phone so that she could pretend she was in bed asleep. Being deceived by someone you love is very hurtful and causes so much pain. Although, I probably didn't have the right to feel that way after deceiving her so many times, it still hurt. What we had was so misguided and confused, we inflicted so much pain on each other and ourselves. It was like trying to soothe pain with a hammer or find company and comfort behind enemy lines. It was like a never-ending story of adultery, deceit, and more pain, and yet somehow love.

When we moved to Aberdeen Proving Ground, Maryland, she would lie and say she was taking trips to meet up with her girlfriend but instead was visiting other men. Because of her lying and sneaking around, I had affairs also. As I said earlier, I was going to do me regardless of what it may cost. In my mind every action deserves a reaction.

Chapter 7

UNAPOLOGETIC MADNESS

One my wife came home from work and asked me what I was doing at a hotel. I told her I wasn't at a hotel, I was at the library. I later found out that a neighbor told her that she saw my truck at a hotel, and she thought me and my wife were there together. I was at the hotel, but I continued to deny it.

In time, we moved back to Fort Hood, Texas. From there, I was eventually deployed to Afghanistan. While in Afghanistan my mind was all over the place, but there wasn't anything I could do. I looked for mail every week, and if I didn't receive any, I got depressed. Nevertheless, I had to move on and stay strong for myself and my fellow soldiers. The internet became our source of communication. RPGs continued to fly over our camp as we scrambled to take cover. Every day was like a nightmare, as we continued to scan vehicles and Afghan personnel for IEDs.

Finally, I returned home and was sent to another unit at Fort Hood. That's when I found out about her and the pastor of the church that we served at in Germany. I was on the Deacon Board and that really pushed me to total numbness. How can you be a helper to a man who serves God, and he and your wife are sending each other perverted messages. Like I stated, I am not a saint, and not claiming to be one, but there are some lines that I would never cross. She said, "He is human just like us." When I confronted him, he was man enough to apologize for what he did. I told him if I ever crossed him again that I was going to slap the mess out of him! She never apologized for anything that she ever did in our marriage, so it's no surprise that she had no apology for this either.

I prayed to God on numerous occasions to show me my wife's evil ways and He did just that. One day, I received an email from an anonymous person. In it was my wife's username and password to her yahoo and military accounts. It also had many messages between her and another man while she was a contractor in Iraq, which was for a year and a half. I confronted her about the emails, she denied them. I told her I had all the information and evidence in front of me. I opened her account once more, and she had just written a new email to one of the men saying, "I need you to contact me as soon as possible because my husband has seen the emails." I confronted her again about the message she had just sent, and all hell broke loose! She claimed that I was breaking into her accounts. I can't break in if the information was provided to me. Rumors began to pour in about her and relationships with men. She even called the man she was sleeping with to try and convince me that they had nothing going on.

Next thing I knew, she was trying to say that I gave her herpes. I told her I didn't have it and never did. I went to sick-call that next morning just to convince her that I didn't have it. The doctor examined me and said, "Staff Sergeant Lott, you do not have herpes." Immediately, I called her to let her know and told her she needed to find someone else to blame because it didn't come from me. She told me later that day that it was a bad yeast infection. She used to always tell me that I was giving her a bacterial infection, but the whole time it was coming from the multiple partners she and I had. She ended up losing a friend in Aberdeen, Maryland because she was told that my wife had sex with her husband while working in Iraq. I had become so numb, I just didn't care anymore and continued having affairs of my own. One thing I learned is that the pot can't be mad with the kettle.

Once she returned home, she slept in the guest room. She was upset because every dime she made was gone, and I wasn't a contributing factor to it. She never knew how to stop spending money. One morning, we were arguing so badly, I took my wedding ring off and threw it at her. The madness never stopped for us.

Chapter 8

FIGHTNING A LOSING BATTLE

Later, we moved to Hawaii. I continued to have an affair and she tried everything possible to end my career. One day, she came home from work, checked the phone log, and saw where I had used the *67 code to make my number private to a particular number. When she asked me about the number, I told her it was a soldier's number and I disabled it so it wouldn't show up on their phone. She called the number but never received an answer. She tried calling it several times, until the number could no longer be reached.

She decided to pull our phone logs and saw that I had been calling that number a lot. Then she took my phone and went into the guest room and wouldn't let me in. I was able to unlock the door. I went in and asked her where my phone was. I proceeded towards her, lifted the mattress, and grabbed my phone. As I was grabbing my phone, she started kicking and hitting me.

Things continued to escalate. She jumped out of the bed, ran into the kitchen, and grabbed a knife. I ran into the bathroom and locked the door. At that moment, I began to call her a she-devil, a hypocrite, and a compulsive liar. I shouted, "Stop acting like a bitch!" She shouted back, "Your mother is a bitch!" Without thinking, I allowed my mouth to control my mind and lashed out, "Your mom is the one in the hospital and I hope she dies!" To this day, this continues to haunt me. I allowed her to take me to the point of no return. When I realized what I said out of anger, I apologized immediately. I called her sister crying and apologized to her as well. I was going to call her brothers and apologize to them also, but they told me not to. Her sister said, "I know you didn't mean it and I accept your apology." I told her that her sister was always saying negative things about my siblings, mother, and stepfather, but I had never said anything negative about her mother. My mother-in-law always treated me like her own. I loved her the same way I loved my mother. There was nothing I wouldn't do for her then and there's nothing I wouldn't do for her today.

We went walking one day to talk about everything and get whatever was on our chest out in the open. Instead of talking, it was more arguing and blaming each other for our failing marriage. She admitted to having an affair and shouted, "It was good too!" This came out of anger. I was shocked and devastated at the same time. I looked at her and replied, "I forgive you because you forgave me when I had my affair." But it didn't remove the hurt I felt, especially because of the way she told me.

She went on to tell me that our daughter told her that when we were stationed in Germany, I had her in bed with me watching a football game, while I was having sex with a woman. I told her that was totally untrue. I told her the same daughter told me that she was talking to a man in Hawaii while she was in the car with her. Also, our other daughter told me she was talking on the phone with the guy she met in Iraq while visiting family in Georgia. She decided to do her own investigation and did the most unexplainable thing. Somehow, she got the Enlisted Record Brief of the female she claimed I was having an affair with. This was personal and sensitive material to have. Now here we go again! Only this time, she was in a predicament that would cause her to lose her government job. As usual, she continued to blame me for everything that was happening. Her friend tried to give me the documents, but I refused to accept them. I knew the magnitude of trouble having those documents could cause and I wanted nothing to do with them. I was at a loss for words, wondering why she would be trying to pass the documents off to me. Her friend turned the documents into the Criminal Investigation Department to clear her of any wrongdoing. I paid $32,000 for a lawyer to help her fight the case. Sadly, it was all for nothing because the evidence was as clear as day.

Time went on and we tried to work things out, but it just wasn't working. We continued to argue more and more. I recall, one Saturday night we were hanging out with our neighbors, who lived directly behind us. I was tired and decided to go home and go to bed. I awoke with her coming into our bedroom asking me to come back to the neighbor's house and have sex with them. I told her, "Hell No! I'm not going over there to do that." When I saw my neighbor the next day, he told me he looked out the kitchen door and saw my wife and his wife kissing. He told me that he couldn't allow that to happen because he considered me a good friend.

On another occasion, our next-door neighbors had a little birthday gathering for the husband and we were all drinking and hanging out in my backyard. I decided to go in the house and call it a night, but she decided to go over to the neighbor's house and give him a lap dance. I couldn't understand why.

Shortly after, I ended up going to Fort Irwin, California for training, which lasted 45 days. I called her one day to check on her and the kids. After we talked, I just put my phone down thinking she would hang up, but she didn't. I looked at my phone and wondered why she didn't hang up. So, I started having a conversation with the guys and said only for a joke that I'd been with four to five women within 24-hours. That was the wrong thing to do. I didn't realize that was not a joke to play with. Immediately, I received a call from my mom saying, "You got caught up, I hear." When I picked up the phone, I knew it was going to be a long day and night.

After the completion of my training at Fort Irwin, I returned to Hawaii and the arguing continued. Sadly to say, I came home from work one day and there was a letter laying in the middle of the bed that said she no longer wanted to be in Hawaii, and she apologizes for the affair she had in Iraq. I was served divorce papers on two occasions while serving in the Army. I told myself to hang in there until I retired, and soon it would all be over. The rumors continued about us. We were toxic to each other. We were two imperfect people doing our best to have a perfect marriage.

Chapter 9

THE BEGINNING OF THE END

Now, she was back in Georgia, and I was in Hawaii finishing my tour. We continued to stay in contact because although the girls were grown, we still had a son that needed both of his parents. By this time, I had almost 25 years of service. She decided she wanted to buy a house back home where we were raised to be closer to our daughters and grandkids. I told her that I thought we were going to buy a home in Texas, but she wanted that house in Georgia. So, I bought the house and we agreed to stay there until our son graduated from high school, and then think about moving. To be honest, I cannot remember us ever reconciling our marriage during that time. Trying to better myself, I began going to counseling before I left Hawaii in 2016.

I flew my wife and son back to Hawaii because they were on my orders for Texas. While there, she decided to connect with one of her lesbian friends and hang out. I knew something was going on with them, but I didn't care. I moved to Texas to do my last and final tour. I continued counseling there. I would go home to Georgia during holidays and long weekends to spend time with my family and make sure the home I had just purchased was ready to move in. She found a small job and I would give her money so she could continue to enjoy herself with family and friends.

However, the money I was giving her was never enough. I was renovating our new home, without any financial support from her, paying for an apartment in Texas, and paying the mortgage on our new home, along with all the other bills at both places. Still, she was never satisfied with what I was able to spare.

I received a call from her one night, saying one of her female friends asked her to come stay with her at a hotel for the weekend. I asked her why she needed her to stay with her? She said because she's there by herself. I told her okay if that was what she wanted to do. As time went by, I asked her friend about that night. She said, yes, my wife stayed with her that night, that said she needed a break. She said she snored all night long. I said, "A break, a break from what?"

When we talked about that night again, she stated they had separate rooms and that she paid for them.

Eventually, I came home from Texas to visit my family. Everything was going well until it was time for me to fly back to Texas. My wife told me she was going up the street because she was not sleepy, and she wanted to drink a little more. When I awakened early the next morning, she was not anywhere to be found in the house. I continued to get dressed because I could not miss my flight, and I had a two-and-a-half-hour drive to the airport. My wife had spent the night up the street at her cousin's boyfriend's house. Her excuse was she had too much to drink and fell asleep. I argued all the way to Atlanta airport and did not care how she got back home.

My wife never had to pay any bills while we were married. The only thing she ever had to pay was the bills she created with her credit cards. I did not realize how many cards she had and how much debt she was in until I retired. She also had a card in my name that I was unaware of. After retiring, she told me I needed to get a job and stop hanging around the house doing nothing. I had not even been retired a full year, or had the time needed to destress from years of such a high paced schedule in the Army. All I wanted to do was hunt, fish, have two dogs, and some chickens. I retired a 100% disabled veteran, with work capabilities, and my pension. She worked from home, and I started substitute teaching at the local middle and high school. You might say, I made her a spoiled little brat. Before retiring, I went to her and told her, "Baby,

I am about to retire, and I will need you to help pay some of the bills until my pension and disability kick in. Without hesitation, she stated, "I have never helped you pay bills and I'm not going to start, you better make a way." I looked at her and said to myself, what have I really gotten myself into with this woman. I was the backbone for my family, and I couldn't get any help from my wife. I could never save money because she would drain the account whenever I tried. She would say, "Save for what, you only live once and you can't take it with you when you die."

Over time, her debts grew larger, and she began to put a lot of stress on me. Then she started working for a company out of Cincinnati. Her income was in the high five digits. I began to get into politics, and she began looking for a job for me. She never supported me with anything I wanted to do. I became a member of our local Lions Club. I was also one of the Board of Directors for the Chamber of Commerce. Eventually, I decided to run for a seat on the City Council. She was against me running. When I told her a local editor wanted to do an article on me and take a family photo of us, I couldn't believe she got so mad. Do you know she had me reschedule the photo shoot three times? When the photo was finally taken, she refused to be in the picture. She packed her bags and left our home for a month.

I can't say that I was surprised at her non-support, because when I would take on difficult tasks to advance my career, she would tell me that I wouldn't succeed in the military. I was told I was worthless, wasn't about shit, dumb, stupid, a bitch ass nigga, a pussy ass nigga, and a terrible husband. I was always being talked down to, or talked at and not to, belittled and degraded by her. On numerous occasions, she'd say to me, "If I only knew." Whatever that was supposed to mean... I took it as she had men lined up to take my place at any given time. I would say to her, "Well if they had to live with you, they would be very disappointed." One thing I can say is that I never deviated from my responsibilities as a father or husband. I was the one who taught all three of my kids how to cook, drive, and manage their finances. I helped them with their homework, attended their school functions, and went to parent/teacher conferences.

I recall my wife going to an interview and declining the job offer. They wanted to hire someone for a program they were trying to get off the ground. Fortunately, it was the exact thing I was doing in the military, so I proudly accepted the position. Not long after, she began to think I was having an affair with someone at my job. I was not having an affair with anyone; I was just going to lunch with a group of co-workers. She called me during my lunch break one day and asked who I was with. I told her who I was with, and she was furious. She came to the restaurant and told me to come outside with her. We got in her truck, and she began to hit and kick me, saying I was sleeping with one of the females. I tried to explain what was going on, but she refused to listen. One of the females came out to explain it was an innocent co-worker's luncheon, which didn't help.

Unfortunately, our marriage didn't make it to our son's graduation. She walked out of our home in 2019 on Christmas eve. She would come by occasionally to shower and change clothes, then off she would go into the world. I told her, "Don't come here taking showers, take it wherever you are laying at night." She let me know that she wanted everything that she bought and said, "I am divorcing you." A few days went by, then I gave her a call to find out when she was coming to get her things. Without really saying when, she stated, "I am going to get them." She waited until I went to work to come and take everything she wanted. I came home to a half empty home. I replaced every piece of furniture that was taken and continued to move on with my life. I was served divorce papers in February of 2020, which I didn't contest and signed on the dotted line.

Now, you would think it was over, but it wasn't. She came back to get things I had set aside in the garage. I told my son not to let her in the house and he said okay. I heard her in the background saying, "Don't no one want to go in your house." Moments later, she came back when no one was home and tried to get in with her key, but I had changed the locks. She broke my bedroom window and proceeded into the house and took other items. My motion sensor and camera picked her up and I called the police to meet me at my home. She was arrested but not charged because the divorce wasn't final, so legally she could still come there. Not long after, she reached out to her lawyer before the judge had the opportunity to sign our divorce papers and had them rescinded. I was served with another set of divorce papers from another lawyer. This time, I contested the documents and retained a lawyer to help with the legal documents.

As time went by, she continued to cause me all types of problems and tried to destroy my character and reputation. The things that came out of her mouth were unbelievable and very disgusting. She sent me numerous text messages saying horrible things to me. One of her very many messages alluded to me being sexually abused by my brother and stepdad, while his friends molested my sisters. There were plenty more horrible messages, which I refuse to share due to the content. I never disrespected her or her family the way she disrespected me during our marriage and divorce proceedings.

Chapter 10
NEVER ENDING STORY

As I mentioned, I moved on with my life and was now engaged. Yet, by any means my ex-wife tried her best to turn friends and her family against me. She would play phone tag, take pictures of my fiancée's car and license plate. She started posting and showing pictures of my fiancée all over social media. There was nothing I could do legally besides wait it out. She would text, call, and email me daily. I would constantly tell her to stop all contact with me. Everyone was in an uproar due to my actions, but I didn't care at all. How could you break into the home where your son resides and leave it unprotected because of the window you broke. It took almost a month to replace the window and repair the damages she caused. If I had broken into her residence, I guarantee you I would have been thrown underneath the jail.

The saga just wouldn't end... Our son's graduation night from high school was his and my worst day ever. I tried to sit on the graduation field with her, but I just couldn't bring myself to do it. I called my son and asked him if he wanted me to sit on the field with his mother. Even though I didn't want to, I would do it for him. He said, "Daddy you don't have to, ask my uncle." Instead, my daughter sat on the graduation field with her mother. Before the graduation was over completely, my wife at that time snatched my son's diploma from our daughter and wouldn't give it back. Now, I'm dealing with trying to retrieve my son's diploma from her. She was escorted off the field to her car as if I was going to try and harm her in some way. I shouted, "Give my son back his diploma!" She shouted, "No, because you want it!" Prior to graduation, I spoke with the principal, and he spoke with the school superintendent about me not wanting to sit with my wife on the graduation field. They refused to accommodate my wishes.

I was going through counseling and seeing a psychiatrist for PTSD, anxiety, depression, insomnia, and marital issues at the time. She was never happy with what I wanted to do with my life after the military. Later, she let me know that I was only a good provider and not a good husband. One of our friends came forth and told me she took my wife to have an abortion when I was deployed to Iraq. How awful can a person be… An abortion, really! This friend was willing to be a witness on my behalf in court. When I brought this news to her attention, her response was, "OK" and laughter. She never once denied the allegation but reached out to the individual by message and said all sorts of bad things to her. I found out she was also being flown out to meet up with her male lovers.

Chapter 11

THE CONCLUSION OF THE MATTER

I know the wrongdoing I have done and the reasons for our divorce, and I'm not afraid to talk about it with anyone. However, she continues to put all the blame on me and only tells what she wants people to know and think. We were finally divorced on 20 August 2021.

Remember, even though we had a big age gap between us, her mom approved of us dating as long as I followed her rules. She was 13 and I was 17 years old. In the end there was a rumor out claiming that she told people I was a sexual predator for dating her at such an early age, and I married her because if I didn't, I would have gone to jail.

I never understood why she had to tell so many lies, when she was the one who left me and our son and served me with divorce papers two months later. All I did was sign on the dotted line. As I said, she tried to discredit me and my family's character, and to turn her family and our friends against me. There were even people I didn't even know that disliked me because of what she told them. I was receiving phone calls from friends in Texas, Maryland, Virginia, and Georgia because of things she told them. She even had her sister and younger brother mad at me and it almost turned into a fight.

Eventually, they realized I was not the enemy in the situation and contacted me to apologize for interfering. I understood their intent as siblings wanting to protect their sister. I recall receiving a few missed calls from a guy that I had never met or seen. I asked my kids if they knew the guy. Finally, I decided to return his call. When we spoke, I told him who I was and asked what his business was with me. He told me that he and my ex-wife had been messing around for about two years, how crazy she was, and what she had done to him. He said if I didn't believe him, then how did he know that she offered me sex when we were going through our divorce, and I turned her down twice. He said he kicked her out of his house. I was shocked and at a loss for words at that moment. I told him, I would have never told anyone that and now she was his problem and not mine anymore.

All I wanted was for everything to stop and to be left out of everything she had going on in her life. I was never a violent person; I believe except for true self-defense for one's life, there is never an excuse for putting your hands on anyone. However, I can count two times that I put my hands on her in a harmful manner. When she said my first daughter didn't belong to me, and when she turned our 20-gallon fish tank over on our second daughter soaking her with water, I lost it. It all started when she walked into the house and saw me on the phone. She asked me who I was talking to, and I told her it was one of my friends. She didn't believe me and tried to call the number back. From there things escalated and she turned over the fish tank. That night, I was furious! I could have taken her head off her shoulders! As she walked out of the house, I walked behind her with an open hand and was about to slap her in the back of the head but before my hand could connect, she turned around and I hit her in the face by mistake. I'm not proud of either time I put my hands on her.

It seems during my years in the Army that I was more concerned about my career than my family. I learned as a Non-commissioned Officer that my problems were less important to my superior officers than their soldiers. If their soldier failed, they also failed. I had the responsibility of taking on everyone's problems except my own. How was it that if one of my soldiers received a DUI, failed the Army fitness test, got a speeding ticket, or ended up in jail over the weekend, I was mostly to blame. My superior would punish me and sometimes remove me from my position of authority.

Chapter 12

NEW LIFE

Now, it was August 18, 2022, and it still had not stopped. I was engaged to a very wonderful, caring, and loving woman. We officially met on social media on 14 February 2020. My divorce papers were signed, and I was just waiting on the judge's signature for it to be final. I had seen her several times before, but I never approached or reached out to her. She and her brother had a hair shop where I got my hair cut. My ex-wife was telling everyone that me and my fiancée were messing around while I was still with her, which is not true at all. When we met, my fiancée was also going through a divorce. I told her she was the one and couldn't explain why. I know God had his hand in it all.

Counseling saved my life and helped me regain love for myself and those very important to me. My ex-wife even reached out to my fiancée's ex-husband, questioning him about her, and telling him about my relationship with his ex-wife. Me and my fiancée were furious with such nonsense. I asked myself, when would it ever end for me? There were times during my marriage when I had suicidal thoughts. The amount of stress and the state of depression I was in was just that great. As I mentioned earlier, I had gotten to the point where I didn't want to go home and deal with the issues and stress that was waiting for me. I made up excuses to stay at work. My mind started playing tricks on me, telling me I would be better off dead. I would question my options, should I run off a bridge into the river, hit an oncoming car or a tree. I found myself sitting at my brother-in-law's grave crying out to him, "What should I do, what should I do!" I was a lost and very unhappy person. Nevertheless, I did what I thought was best for my kids, which was to stay and raise them. I never wanted another man raising my kids, so I hung in there.

Life can be incredibly stressful and cruel when you can't live up to other's expectations. I thought I was doing everything right in the beginning of our marriage, only to find out it was all wrong. Marriage is a sacred commitment between two people, who love each other so much that it hurts them to see the other one hurt. I was always a rational person and would evaluate myself before being hypocritical or blaming others for my sadness.

In life, we battle demonic forces daily, those spirits within the universe that move among us all, and those personal demons within us. There are no perfect people and there never will be. However, we can learn from our past, endeavor to better ourselves, and embrace the future with hope and determination. There is so much out there to learn, explore, and experience when we refuse to give up on ourselves. I learned without love for yourself, you can't show love to others. Learning to love myself has been one of my greatest accomplishments. Understand, love is a dangerous emotion that should be handled carefully and respectfully, not played with like a game. If love is not treated right, there will be heartache and pain. Know your worth... because if a man's worth is based on pleasing others, he will always feel guilty when doing anything for himself. I am working on forgiveness every day of my life for the pain I caused my ex-wife, kids, family, friends, and myself.

I cannot say this enough, counseling is a tool that I believe everyone should use in a time of crisis and need for healing. For far too long, within our culture there has been a negative stigma of being called crazy associated with receiving counselling and therapy. I am a living witness that is totally untrue. Counseling helped to prepare me for what was coming in my life and reconnect me with the world. I saw myself getting better every day, and I grew more and more determined. I refused to give up. Never give up and never stop smiling. It is my prayer that me, my family, those around me, and you and your family continue to be blessed in the name of Jesus. Amen.

Oh yeah, I am still seeing a psychiatrist, and continuing to seek and thank God in all that I do. Also, I have two dogs and I go fishing and hunting just as I wanted. Yes, I can be who God predestined me to be, and with the help and support of my new wife to be, Octavia Denise King Lott, every day I'm becoming that man.

BATTLE JOURNAL

Journal your Battles: Past and Present

Battle Journal: _____

_____

_____

_____

_____

_____

_____

_____

_____

_____

_____

_____

_____

_____

_____

_____

_____

_____

_____

_____

Battle Journal: _____

_____

_____

_____

_____

_____

_____

_____

_____

_____

_____

_____

_____

_____

_____

_____

_____

_____

_____

_____

_____

Battle Journal: _____

_____

_____

_____

_____

_____

_____

_____

_____

_____

_____

_____

_____

_____

_____

_____

_____

_____

_____

_____

_____

_____

Battle Journal: _____

_____

_____

_____

_____

_____

_____

_____

_____

_____

_____

_____

_____

_____

_____

_____

_____

_____

_____

_____

_____

Battle Journal: _____

_____

_____

_____

_____

_____

_____

_____

_____

_____

_____

_____

_____

_____

_____

_____

_____

_____

_____

_____

_____

_____

Battle Journal: _____

_____

_____

_____

_____

_____

_____

_____

_____

_____

_____

_____

_____

_____

_____

_____

_____

_____

_____

_____

_____

_____

Battle Journal: _____

_____

_____

_____

_____

_____

_____

_____

_____

_____

_____

_____

_____

_____

_____

_____

_____

_____

_____

_____

_____

_____

Battle Journal: _____

_____

_____

_____

_____

_____

_____

_____

_____

_____

_____

_____

_____

_____

_____

_____

_____

_____

_____

_____

_____

_____